Theory Paper   Grade 8   2024   A

Duration 3 hours

Candidates should answer all FIVE questions.
Write your answers on this paper – no others will be accepted.
Answers must be written clearly and neatly – otherwise marks may be lost.

RKS

1   Complete the violin parts in the following extract adapted from a trio sonata by Corelli, following
the figuring shown under the basso continuo.

15

3

2 Complete the given outline of the following passage, adapted from a piano piece by Mendelssohn (1809–1847). Note that most of the left-hand part is in the treble clef.

Allegretto

etc.

3 Compose a complete melody of not less than 12 bars using **ONE** of the following openings and for the given unaccompanied instrument. Continue in the same style and include appropriate performance directions. Write the complete melody on the staves below.

VIOLIN

BASSOON

4 Look at the extract printed opposite, which is from a song by Wolf, and then answer the questions below.

25

(a) Give the meaning of:

Mässig .... (2)

langsam .... (2)

(b) Complete these statements:

(i) The soprano and left-hand piano part sound a note in unison in bar .... (2)

(ii) There is a lower auxiliary note in the right-hand piano part in bar .... (2)

(iii) There is a melodic interval of an
augmented 2nd in the bottom left-hand part in bars .... (2)

(c) Identify the shaded chords marked ∗ in bars 2 and 4 by writing on the dotted lines below. Use either words or symbols. For each chord, indicate the position and show whether it is major, minor, augmented or diminished.

Bar 2 .... ⎫ (3)
                                                    ⎬ Key   E♭ minor
Bar 4 .... ⎭ (3)

(d) Compare the bracketed sections of the **piano part** of bar 8 with bar 10 (both marked ⌐‾‾‾‾¬) and then name four differences.

Differences   1   .... (1)

              2   .... (1)

              3   .... (1)

              4   .... (1)

(e) Answer TRUE or FALSE to this statement:

There are **no** rising chromatic semitones
(augmented unisons) in the right-hand piano part in this extract.   .... (2)

(f) Name three features of the music that contribute to the change of mood at bar 12.

1   .... (1)

2   .... (1)

3   .... (1)

5 Look at the extract printed on pages 9–10, which is from a symphony, and then answer the
questions below.

25

(a) Give the meaning of:

allargando .... (2)

a 2 (e.g. bar 2, flutes) .... (2)

arco (e.g. bar 3, cellos) .... (2)

(b) (i) Write out the part for **first** clarinet in bars 3–4 as it would sound at concert pitch.

Clarinet 1 (4)

(ii) Using the blank stave at the foot of page 10, write out the part for **first** horn in bar 9 as it
would sound at concert pitch. (2)

(c) Complete these statements:

(i) On the first note of bar 5, the instrument
sounding in unison with the double basses is the .... (2)

(ii) The cellos have to use an open string in bar .... (2)

(d) Answer TRUE or FALSE to this statement:

The third trombone and tuba sound in unison in bar 7. .... (2)

(e) Describe fully the numbered and bracketed harmonic intervals **sounding** between:

1 first clarinet and flutes, bar 2 .... (2)

2 first and second bassoons, bar 4 .... (2)

3 first trombone and first horn, bar 9 .... (2)

(f) From the list below, underline one period during which this piece was written.

1700–1800   1800–1900   1900–2000 (1)

8

(b) (ii)
bar 9

Horn 1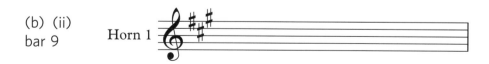

10

Theory Paper   Grade 8   2024   B

Duration 3 hours

Candidates should answer all **FIVE** questions.
Write your answers on this paper – no others will be accepted.
Answers must be written clearly and neatly – otherwise marks may be lost.

1 Complete the violin parts in the following extract adapted from a trio sonata by Corelli, following the figuring shown under the basso continuo.

15

2 Complete the given outline of the following passage, adapted from a piano piece by
Schubert (1797–1828).

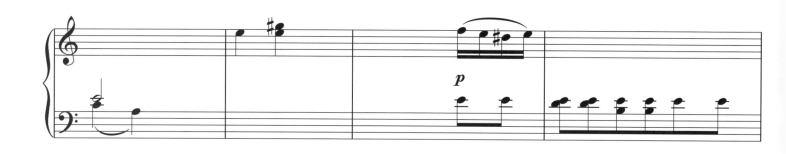

3 Compose a complete melody of not less than 12 bars using **ONE** of the following openings and for the given unaccompanied instrument. Continue in the same style and include appropriate performance directions. Write the complete melody on the staves below.

VIOLIN

Con moto

Grieg

p

TROMBONE

Deciso

f

Menuetto

Moderato e grazioso

Trio

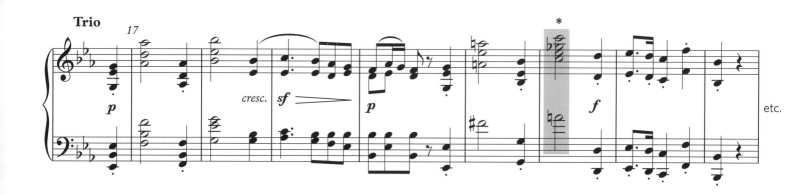

4 Look at the extract printed opposite, which is from a piano sonata, and then answer the questions below.

(a) Give the meaning of **grazioso**. .... (2)

(b) Identify the shaded chords marked ∗ in bars 11 (ignoring the ornament) and 22 by writing on the dotted lines below. Use either words or symbols. For each chord, indicate the position and show whether it is major, minor, augmented or diminished.

Bar 11 .... Key E♭ major (3)

Bar 22 .... Key B♭ major (3)

(c) Complete these statements:

(i) There is syncopation in the right-hand part in bar .... (2)

(ii) There is a two-bar tonic pedal note
(not sustained) in the inner right-hand part in bars .... (2)

(iii) There is a melodic interval of a minor 9th in the top right-hand part in bars .... (2)

(iv) There is a chromatic lower auxiliary note in the left-hand part in bar .... (2)

(d) Write out in full the top right-hand part of bar 9 as it should be played. Part of the bar is given.

(3)

(e) Answer TRUE or FALSE to these statements:

(i) In bars 9–16, the smallest harmonic interval
between the right-hand and left-hand parts is a major 3rd. .... (2)

(ii) The last note in the right-hand part of bar 1 is a note of anticipation. .... (2)

(f) Give two reasons which suggest that Beethoven is the composer of this extract.

1 .... (1)

2 .... (1)

5 Look at the extract printed on pages 17–18, which is from the third movement of Tchaikovsky's *Manfred* Symphony, and then answer the questions below.

(a) Give the meaning of:

a 2 (e.g. bar 3, oboes) .... (2)

𝄽. (e.g. bar 6, timpani) .... (2)

⊓ (e.g. bar 5, cellos) .... (2)

(b) (i) Write out the parts for first and second horns in bar 1 as they would sound at concert pitch.

(2)

(ii) Write out the part for **second** clarinet in bar 5 as it would sound at concert pitch.

(2)

(c) Describe fully the numbered and bracketed harmonic intervals **sounding** between:

1 first and second
bassoons and bass clarinet, bar 3 .... (2)

2 second clarinet and cor anglais, bar 6 .... (2)

3 violas and second horn, bar 8 .... (2)

(d) Complete these statements:

(i) On the first note of bar 1, the instruments **sounding** in unison with the second oboe

are the .... and the .... (2)

(ii) On the first note of bar 6, the instruments **sounding** an octave higher than the double basses

are the ...., the ....

and the .... (3)

(e) Answer TRUE or FALSE to these statements:

(i) The second violin and viola parts do **not** cross in this extract. .... (2)

(ii) The chord formed by the notes sounding on the
first note of bar 9 is an Italian augmented 6th chord. .... (2)

16

Theory Paper   Grade 8   2024   C

TOTAL MARKS
100

Duration 3 hours

Candidates should answer all FIVE questions.
Write your answers on this paper – no others will be accepted.
Answers must be written clearly and neatly – otherwise marks may be lost.

1 Complete the oboe parts in the following extract adapted from a trio sonata by Colista, following the figuring shown under the basso continuo.

15

2 Complete the given outline of the following passage, adapted from a piano piece by Reinecke (1824–1910). Note the left-hand part is in the treble clef throughout.

3 Compose a complete melody of not less than 12 bars using **ONE** of the following openings and for the given unaccompanied instrument. Continue in the same style and include appropriate performance directions. Write the complete melody on the staves below.

FLUTE

HORN (at concert pitch)

4 Look at the extract printed opposite, which is from a piano sonata by Schubert, and then answer
the questions below.

(a) Compare bar 6 with bar 7 (both marked ⌐━━━━━┐) and then name two similarities and
two differences.

Similarities   1   .... (1)

2   .... (1)

Differences   1   .... (1)

2   .... (1)

(b) Identify the shaded chords marked ∗ in bars 4 and 11 by writing on the dotted lines below. Use either
words or symbols. For each chord, indicate the position and show whether it is major, minor, augmented
or diminished.

Bar 4   ....   ⎞ (3)
                                                                                        ⎬   Key   E major
Bar 11   ....   ⎠ (3)

(c) Complete these statements:

(i)   There is a rising chromatic semitone
(augmented unison) in the inner left-hand part in bars .... (2)

(ii)   There is a V⁷–I progression in the relative minor key in bar .... (2)

(iii) The largest melodic interval in
the bottom left-hand part is a(n) .... (2)

(iv)   There is a three-bar dominant pedal note (not sustained) in bars .... (2)

(d) Write out in full the top right-hand part of bar 14 as it should be played. Part of the bar is given.

(3)

(e) Answer TRUE or FALSE to these statements:

(i)   The notes sounding on the final quaver of bar 3 form a diminished 7th chord.   .... (2)

(ii)   The harmonic intervals of a 6th on the last three quavers of bar 8 are all minor.   .... (2)

5 Look at the extract printed on pages 25–26, which is from the first movement of Scriabin's Symphony No. 2, and then answer the questions below.

(a) Give the meaning of:

unis. (e.g. bar 5, first violins) .... (2)

$\overset{\circ}{\underset{\equiv}{}}$ (e.g. bar 7, first violins) .... (2)

+ (e.g. bar 7, horns) .... (2)

(b) Answer TRUE or FALSE to this statement:

On the first note of bar 1, there are
no instruments **sounding** in unison with the first clarinet. .... (2)

(c) Using the blank staves at the foot of page 26, write out:

(i) the part for first clarinet in bar 9 as it would sound at concert pitch. (2)

(ii) the part for **first** horn in bar 11 as it would sound at concert pitch. (2)

(d) Complete these statements:

(i) On the first note of bar 7, the instruments **sounding** in unison with the top note of the violas

are the .... and the .... (2)

(ii) On the first note of bar 8, the instruments **sounding** in unison with the horns

are the ...., the ....

and the .... (3)

(iii) The viola and cello parts cross in bar(s) .... (2)

(e) Describe fully the numbered and bracketed harmonic intervals **sounding** between:

1 first violins and first trumpet, bar 7 .... (2)

2 double basses (top note) and cellos, bar 9 .... (2)

3 second horn and second bassoon, bar 10 .... (2)

(c) (i)
bar 9
Clarinet 1

(c) (ii)
bar 11
Horn 1

Theory Paper   Grade 8   2024   S

TOTAL MARKS
100

Duration 3 hours

Candidates should answer all FIVE questions.
Write your answers on this paper – no others will be accepted.
Answers must be written clearly and neatly – otherwise marks may be lost.

1   Complete the violin parts in the following extract adapted from a trio sonata by Corelli, following the figuring shown under the basso continuo.

15

2 Complete the given outline of the following passage, adapted from a piano piece by Gurlitt (1820–1901). Note that the left-hand part is in the treble clef throughout.

28

3 Compose a complete melody of not less than 12 bars using **ONE** of the following openings and for the given unaccompanied instrument. Continue in the same style and include appropriate performance directions. Write the complete melody on the staves below.

TRUMPET (at concert pitch)

Berlioz (adapted)

CLARINET (at concert pitch)

Molto moderato

4 Look at the extract printed opposite, which is from a piano piece by Field, and then answer the questions below.

(a) Identify the shaded chords marked * in bars 3 and 5 by writing on the dotted lines below. Use either words or symbols. For each chord, indicate the position and show whether it is major, minor, augmented or diminished.

Bar 3   ....   ⎫   (3)

Bar 5   ....   ⎬   Key   C major   (3)
⎭

(b) Complete these statements:

(i)   There is a simultaneous false (cross) relation between the hands in bar ....   (2)

(ii)   There is a decorated perfect cadence in the dominant key in bars ....   (2)

(iii)   In bars 1–8, the smallest harmonic interval between the hands occurs in bar ....   (2)

(c) Give the full names of the notes of melodic decoration (e.g. changing note) marked **X** (bracketed), **Y** and **Z** in the right-hand part of bars 11, 13 and 14.

X   ....   (2)

Y   ....   (2)

Z   ....   (2)

(d) Write out in full the top right-hand part of bar 5 as it should be played. Part of the bar is given.

(3)

(e) Answer TRUE or FALSE to these statements:

(i)   The music passes through the relative minor key in bars 14–15.   ....   (2)

(ii)   The harmonic intervals of a 6th in the left-hand part of bar 16 are all major.   ....   (2)

5 Look at the extract printed on pages 33–34, which is from Debussy's *Jeux*, and then answer the questions below.

(a) Give the meaning of:

Tambour de Basque .... (2)

sourdines (e.g. bar 1, first violins) .... (2)

Cédez (bar 4) .... (2)

sur la touche (bar 5, first violins) .... (2)

(b) Answer TRUE or FALSE to these statements:

(i) On the first note of bar 2, **no** other
instrument sounds in unison with the third horn. .... (2)

(ii) The highest- and lowest-sounding notes
in this extract have the same letter name. .... (2)

(c) (i) Write out the parts for first and second horns in bar 1 as they would sound at concert pitch.

(2)

(ii) Using the blank stave at the foot of page 34, write out the part for second clarinet in bar 5
as it would sound at concert pitch. (3)

(d) Describe fully the numbered and bracketed harmonic intervals **sounding** between:

1 first bassoon and piccolo, bar 2 .... (2)

2 first trumpet and second flute, bar 4 .... (2)

(e) Complete these statements:

(i) On the third beat of bar 2, there is a note and its enharmonic equivalent sounding

simultaneously between the third bassoon and the .... (2)

(ii) The chord formed by the notes **sounding** in the woodwind section on the first note of bar 4

is a(n) .... chord in .... inversion in the key of B major. (2)

(c) (ii)
bar 5

Clarinet 2